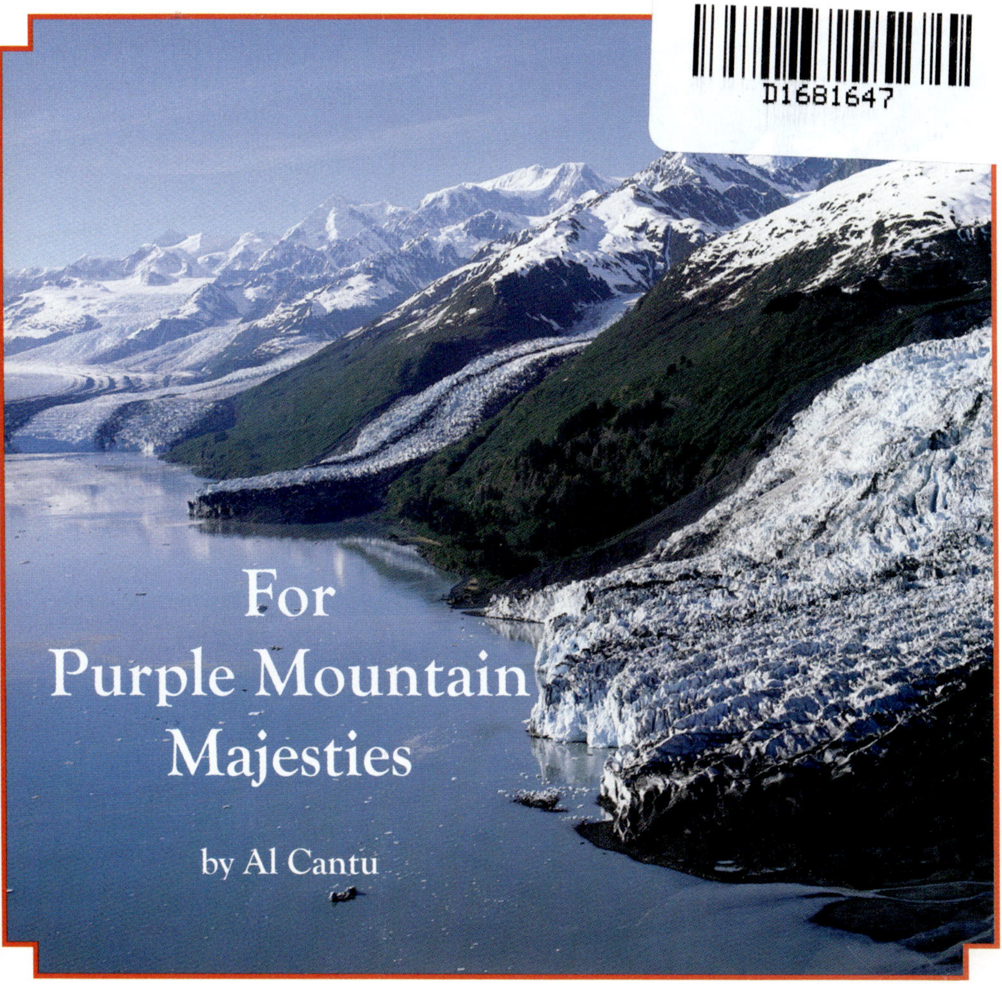

For Purple Mountain Majesties

by Al Cantu

Editorial Offices: Glenview, Illinois • Parsippany, New Jersey • New York, New York
Sales Offices: Needham, Massachusetts • Duluth, Georgia • Glenview, Illinois
Coppell, Texas • Sacramento, California • Mesa, Arizona

About one hundred years ago, a woman wrote a song called "America the Beautiful." Her song was a gift from her heart to the whole United States. When people sing this song, it reminds them of beautiful things in this great land.

"O beautiful for spacious skies,
For amber waves of grain,
For purple mountain majesties
Above the fruited plain!"
— Katharine Lee Bates

---

amber waves of grain: yellow fields of swaying wheat or corn

majesties: power, honor, and greatness

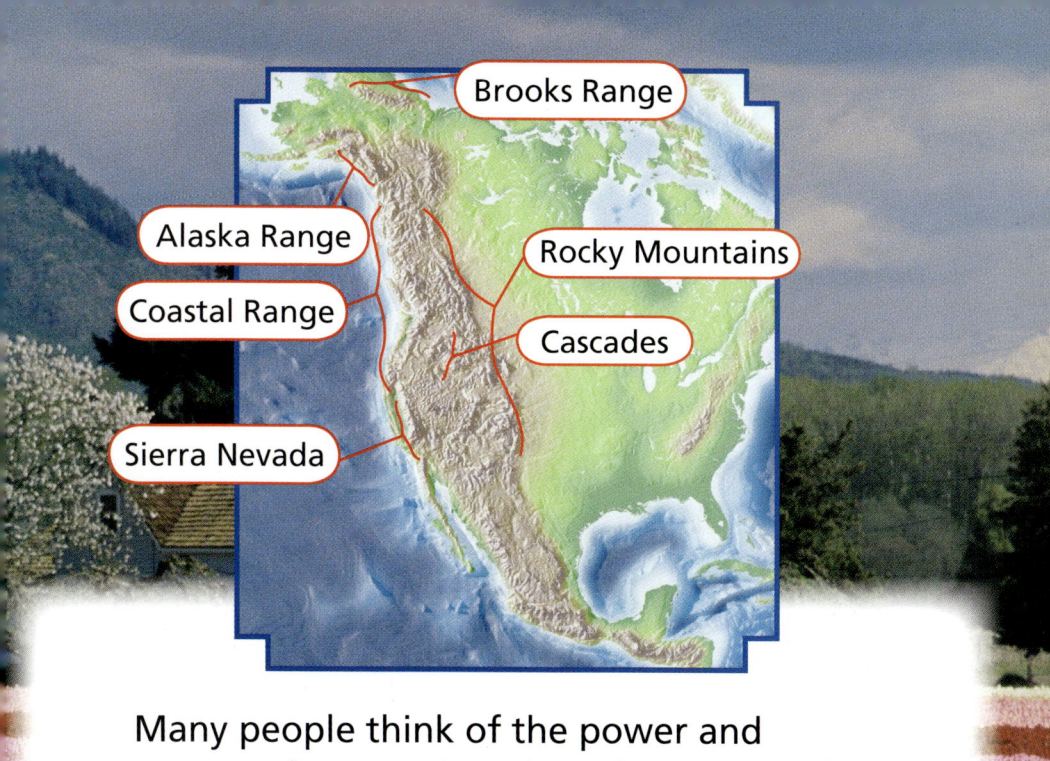

Many people think of the power and greatness of mountains when they see the far West of the United States. The mountains of the far West stand in rows. These rows are called *ranges*. This map shows the main mountain ranges of far Western North America.

| **Extend Language** | **Multiple-Meaning Words** |

Some English words can mean more than one thing. The word *range* can mean "a long row or line of mountains" or "a broad piece of land" or even "a large cooking stove"! It can also be a verb meaning "to wander," as in: *Bears range throughout the Sierra Nevada lands*.

Look at the words in the box. Use a dictionary to find two or three meanings for each word.

| rock | plain | park |

The Brooks Range is in the northern part of Alaska. It runs about 600 miles across Alaska, from east to west.

The highest peaks in the Brooks Range are so high that they are covered with ice and snow most of the year. The snow drains into icy rivers. The rivers flow into icy seas. It's cold up there!

Imagine being on the north side of the Brooks Range. You hike down the slope, and you arrive at the Arctic Coastal Plain. The next stop is the Arctic Ocean! All you hear is the wind. You only see a few large animals like bears and moose. There are no people, except you. You are in the wilderness!

Denali's steep slope rises to more than 20,000 feet above sea level.

The Alaska Range is just south of the Brooks Range. You can see them on the map on page 3. The tallest peak in North America is part of this mountain range. It has two names: *Denali* and *Mount McKinley*. It stands tall at 20,320 feet!

The native people in the far North named this mountain Denali. *Denali* means "high one." Later, it also was named Mount McKinley after an American president. Today, this tall mountain peak stands in Denali National Park in Alaska.

---

native people: the first people to live in the area

Some of the mountains of the Coastal Range are right on the coast.

The Coastal Range runs along the Pacific Coast of North America. It runs from southwestern Alaska to northern California. There are many coastal ranges throughout the world. The word *coast* means "land next to the ocean." So a *coastal range* is any range of mountains next to an ocean.

The mountains of this coastal range are not tall. These highlands include hills as well as peaks. But sitting at the edge of the ocean, the mountains of the Coastal Range are spectacular.

---

spectacular: very beautiful; very impressive

The Cascade Range

The Cascade mountains stretch over 700 miles across southern Canada, Oregon, Washington, and Northern California. A long valley separates them from the Coastal Range. Many of the tall mountains in the Cascade Range are covered with snow. The tallest is Mt. Rainier at 14,410 feet. Mount Rainier is in Washington State.

If you fly above this part of the country on a clear day, you can see a string of mountains. These are the Cascades.

It is believed that Yosemite Valley was formed by a glacier.

The Sierra Nevada runs from northwest to southeast for most of the length of California. Sierra means a chain or range of mountains or hills. The tallest mountain in this range is Mount Whitney, in California. Mount Whitney is 14,495 feet high.

Some of the country's most beautiful national parks are in the Sierra Nevada. Yosemite National Park is in this range. Kings Canyon National Park and Sequoia National Park with their huge Sequoia trees, are there too.

In this book, you have learned about many mountains and mountain ranges. Which ones do you want to visit and explore first?